I AM YOUR PE

FINDING GODS PEACE IN A TROUBLED WORLD

JULIE CLARK

Copyright © 2012, 2013 by TCK Publishing.

For more poetry and testimony and prayers

Photos, friends and links go to

www.freewebs.com/journeyintohope/

WHY I WROTE THIS BOOK

Hi there, thank you for looking at this book and I pray that you will be blessed and encouraged

I am married with two teenaged boys. I have been through many ups and downs in my life but I have always had my faith in God who I know has been loving me and leading me the whole time. Two years ago, I had the privilege of being able to put together a book of some of my poems. The book was called Journey into Hope. One morning I was praying what the next step was in my journey as a writer and he led me to the I am statements of the bible but also the statements that he wants too encourage us with, for examle this book is named I am your peace. Then God gave me some more titles and said it is a series of books rather than one title,

So with joy in my heart and a prayer on my tounge I step boldly out in faith to follow my master and be His mouthpeice and to write what he says to this troubled world

WHY YOU SHOULD READ THIS BOOK

This book will help you read bible verses that complement the title of the book in your hand. The book will be laid out the same way, there will be a bible verse then a poem followed by a thought and finally a short prayer my prayer would be that you would be encouraged and that Gods words would sink into your heart and take root. That on the days where you are being blown about on the stormy seas, you will be able to bring to remembrance the scriptures, poems and thoughts that you have read in book

TABLE OF CONTENTS

Why I Wrote This Book

Why You Should Read This Book

It is well with my soul

Luke 1 v78-79

Job 22:21-30 (NLT)

John 14 v 27

john 16 v 33

Mark 4 v 39

Ephesians 2 v 17

Psalms 62 v 5-7

Psalms 4 v 8

Psalms 85 v 8- 13

IT IS WELL WITH MY SOUL

When peace, like a river, attendeth my way,

When sorrows like sea billows roll;

Whatever my lot, Thou has taught me to say,

It is well, it is well, with my soul

It is well, with my soul,

It is well, it is well, with my soul.

Though Satan should buffet, though trials should come,

Let this blest assurance control,

That Christ has regarded my helpless estate,

And hath shed His own blood for my soul.

My sin, oh, the bliss of this glorious thought!

My sin, not in part but the whole,

Is nailed to the cross, and I bear it no more,

Praise the Lord, praise the Lord, O my soul!

For me, be it Christ, be it Christ hence to live:

If Jordan above me shall roll,

No pang shall be mine, for in death as in life

Thou wilt whisper Thy peace to my soul.

Lord, 'tis for Thee, for Thy coming we wait,

The sky, not the grave, is our goal;

Oh, trump of the angel! Oh, voice of the Lord!

Blessed hope, blessed rest of my soul!

And Lord, haste the day when my faith shall be sight,

The clouds be rolled back as a scroll;

The trump shall resound, and the Lord shall descend,

Even so, it is well with my soul.

BIBLE VERSE

Luke 1 v 78-79

78 A new day will dawn on us from above because our God is loving and merciful.

79 He will give light to those who live in the dark and in death's shadow. He will guide us into the way of peace."

POEM

All is well when we have Gods peace.

Although the road is tough.

We can stand and fight.

In the peace of Jesus Christ.

It's higher than the mountains.

It's deeper than the sea.

God's peace surpasses knowledge.

If we will let it be.

It reaches into sadness.

It reaches into hate.

It reaches things that are too deep.

For us to ever know.

So will you today.

Reach out for God.

And receive his glorious peace.

It's a gift so free and true.

THOUGHT

Although this world is a tough place if we can fix our eyes onto Jesus and accept his love and peace then no matter what we go through we can endure all. He will give is his peace not to make life easy for us but to let us know that we can trust him in all that we go through because he has promised in his word that he will give us his peace.

PRAYER

Heavenly Father I give you praise and lift my hands to you for you are my peace .You are my hiding place, you listen to my heart felt prayer and although the situation that I am facing today may not change, nor does your perfect peace.
Amen

BIBLE VERSE

Job 22:21-30

21 "Submit to God and you will have peace; then things will go well for you.

22 Listen to his instructions, and store them in your heart.

23 If you return to the Almighty, you will be restored— so clean up your life.

24 If you give up your lust for money and throw your precious gold into the river,

25 the Almighty himself will be your treasure. He will be your precious silver!

26 "Then you will take delight in the Almighty and look up to God.

27 You will pray to him, and he will hear you, and you will fulfil your vows to him.

28 You will succeed in whatever you choose to do, and light will shine on the road ahead of you.

29 If people are in trouble and you say, 'Help them,' God will save them. 30 even sinners will be rescued; they will be rescued because your hands are pure."

POEM

Come to me and kneel in peace

While the storms in your life are raging

Leave behind all worries and fears

And kneel before me in peace

Go into that secret place

Where my peace can freely flow

Like a river flowing fast and strong

And feel the warmth of my sun

Feel my peace flooding your life

Washing away all doubt and fear

Filling your heart with hope again

Renewing your life with my love

THOUGHT

Wow what a fantastic scripture. So many times in scripture
we are told if we do something then the Lord will do another.
Sometimes when things go wrong we so easily loose Gods
peace and walk away from him in anger and frustration. But
that is not what God intends for us, he wants to be our peace
permanently because he loves us and wants the best for us.
God wants us to stay in His peace so He can mold and shape

us and bring us through this tough situation that we find ourselves in. Now is the time to pray and enter into worship, to fix our eyes and our hope totally on God, to submit to his leading and trust him. If we can do this then we can know his peace, a peace that passes all understanding

PRAYER

Father God I run into your arms when the world is spinning so fast and there seems no rest. I will take some time to be with you and learn to put all things into your care. You are the author and the finisher of my faith and I know that you will never leave me or forsake me. Amen

BIBLE VERSE

John 14:-27 (ASV)

27 Peace I leave with you; my peace I give unto you: not as the world gives, I give unto you. Let not your heart be troubled, neither let it be fearful.

REST

Rest in my loving Jesus arms

Rest in him he will make no demands

Feel his arms securely around you

Giving you strength and peace anew

See in his eyes a love that is true

Feel his cleansing, making you new

Grow into love and joy untold

And see his purpose for you unfold

He loves the young ones and the old

His love alone more precious than gold

So in his arms and feel the peace

That comes from a love that knows no bounds

Rest in his arms and always be safe

Rest in his arms and you will win the race

Rest in his arms, have a smile on your face

And feel the warmth of his heavenly place

THOUGHT

When the storms of life are raging all around us, we are so blessed to be able to go into a secret place with the Lord and receive his peace. We can leave the world and all its worries at the foot of the cross and renew our strength in peace that only Jesus brings

PRAYER

Father God I pray that you will bring your peace into my life as I lay my worries before you, I know with confidence that you have given me your peace I receive it now in the name of Jesus. Amen

BIBLE VERSE

John 16:33

33 I have told you all this so that you may have peace in me.
Here on earth you will have many trials and sorrows. But
take heart, because I have overcome the world."

POEM

God's peace is like a deep dark cave

In the forest of wild animals

Protecting us from the roaming things

Protecting us from the storms

God's peace is like a hiding place

Full of comfort and of hope

Giving us the strength to carry on

When the road ahead gets tough

God's peace is like a sleeping child

At rest with the world outside

Snuggled softly to the mothers breast

In simple and abounding trust

God's peace is like a harbor

Giving shelter to a boat

The sailor is wise and comes inside

When the winds and storms do blow

So seek Gods peace within your heart

When the times are bleak and cold

Trust in his unfailing love

And he will see you through

THOUGHT

Gods peace is gentle and calm it's not loud and shouting, just as a sleeping baby or a gentle peace, it makes you calm in the midst of the storm, it's your anchor in the storms of life

PRAYER

Jesus let your peace be our anchor in the storm, a baby still and sleeping let the warmth of your love flood our hearts with your peace. Amen

BIBLE VERSE

Mark 4:39

...Jesus Himself was in the stern, asleep on the cushion; and they woke Him and said to Him, "Teacher, do You not care that we are perishing?" And He got up and rebuked the wind and said to the sea, "Hush, be still." And the wind died down and it became perfectly calm. And He said to them, "Why are you afraid? Do you still have no faith?"...

POEM

Be still my fearful heart

Be still my crazed mind

Find your peace

In the Lord and Savior

Find peace in the King of Kings

Be still my troubled breast

Be still my troubled mind

For God has given you

His love everlasting

And that love casts out all fears

I'm tired, oh so tired

Well come unto me my child

Rest for a while

You are held in my arms

And there you know

You have nothing to fear

So rest my child Rest in me

Give up fighting And rest in me

I will guide you I will lead you

On the path I set before you

THOUGHT

We do not have to fear the storms of life with Jesus in our boat, he knows exactly what is happening to us and he has the confidence to know that we will come through the trials we have to go through so let us put our trust in him and feel his everlasting peace

Father God thank you that you are my peace in the midst of stormy sea and all I have to do is trust you that you are with me and that you will calm the storms. Amen

BIBLE VERSE

Ephesians 2:17

and might reconcile them both in one body to God through the cross, by it having put to death the enmity. AND HE CAME AND PREACHED PEACE TO YOU WHO WERE FAR AWAY, AND PEACE TO THOSE WHO WERE NEAR; for through Him we both have our access in one Spirit to the Father.

POEM

The future is safe

I cannot see the future

But all I have to do is trust

My Savior Jesus sees it all

And he will guide me through

I do not know its twists and turns,

Its mountains, valleys and hills.

But I can trust my Jesus.

And He will carry me through.

I do not know its joys and pain

And every emotional high and low

But I know who holds my future

It's Jesus Christ my Lord

So today in faith I will take his hand

And let Him lead me on

Through all the joys and all the sorrow

Until he leads me home

THOUGHT

Although in this world at the moment there is a lot of uncertainty for Christians who have put their trust in Christ we can have the peace in knowing that our future is secure in Christ. He is our living savior, who always leads us and guides us in his way and his truth, and we can trust him no matter what

PRAYER

Heavenly Father Lord and king I give you praise that I am secure in you and that you are leading me every day of my life

PSALMS 62v 5-7

[5] Only God gives inward peace, and I depend on him.
[6] God alone is the mighty rock that keeps me safe, and he is the fortress where I feel secure.
[7] God saves me and honours me. He is that mighty rock where I find safety.

POEM

Peace in our hearts

That's what we pray

Peace in our minds

At the start of the day

Peace as we travel

Through this dry land

Peace to all people

Who take Gods hand

Peace in the valley

In the shadow of death

Peace for the grieving

And those who are bereaved

Peace in the making

When the fighting will end

Peace for a nation

A friendship to mend

True peace it is found

In Jesus alone

When all of our wills

To Jesus have flown

Peace at the ending

Of a long tiring day

Peace in the knowing

Jesus is the only way

THOUGHT

In everything we do in life we have the amazing gift of peace from God, it will help us go through every situation knowing that God is in control, he is watching over us and walking beside us

PRAYER

Thank you heavenly father that you are our peace in every situation we face. That you are watching over us and telling us not to be afraid, help us to trust you and receive the peace that passes all understanding

BIBLE VERSE

PSALMS 4 v 8

There are many who say, "Who will show us *any* good?"
LORD, lift up the light of your countenance upon us.
[7] You have put gladness in my heart, More than in the season
that their grain and wine increased.
[8] I will both lie down in peace, and sleep; For You alone, O
LORD, make me dwell in safety.

POEM

Go in faith and walk with me

Every step throughout the day

I'll be your peace

I'll be your guide

On every step of the way

It may be bad

It may be good

You may see the darkness

But I am your light

I will shine a way before you

When in the valley you walk

So take my hand and walk by faith

And I will lead you all the way

To the end of the path

To that glorious day

Where I will see you face to face

And hold you in my arms

THOUGHT

Gods light is shining upon us and helps us to see his truth and
the way ahead of us. I love this verse as it is now a prayer
that is said at the end of a day

PRAYER

So Lord Jesus tonight as I lay to sleep I will know your peace is all around me and that I am safe in your arms. I need not fear the evil one as angels come and minister around my bed and I will awake renewed and refreshed ready to start a new day. Amen

BIBLE VERSE

Psalm 85:8-13

[8] I will hear what God the LORD will speak, For He will speak peace To His people and to His saints; But let them not turn back to folly.

[9] Surely His salvation *is* near to those who fear Him, That glory may dwell in our land.

[10] Mercy and truth have met together; Righteousness and peace have kissed.

[11] Truth shall spring out of the earth, And righteousness shall look down from heaven.

[12] Yes, the LORD will give *what is* good; And our land will yield its increase.

[13] Righteousness will go before Him, And shall make His footsteps *our* pathway.

POEM

The final surrender

When I see your love for me

Ad all the things you have done

The way you died to set me free

Oh lord I surrender to you

All my pain and all my sorrow

All my worries and my fears

Take my life in this final surrender

And change my heart within

Change the heart that was of tone

Into a heart of flesh and love

Freely you gave your life for me

So freely I surrender to you

The peace I feel as I surrender

Is one I never want to lose

To know that you are in full control

And you will bring me saftly through

Lord this is my final surrender

Its where I will take my stand

O choose to surrender my God and king

I choose, my life. To surrender to you

THOUGHT

When we finally surrender to God and trust him with our lives and all who we love then God fills us with his peace because we are living how God wants us to live

PRAYER

Father God I surrender my life and al that I have and hold dear. Send your peace in fullness and a peace that passes all understanding in your precious name I ask it Amen

About The Author

My name is Julie Clark and I am from Kent UK

I am a born again Christian and I am married with two boys

I have been writing poetry since I was sixteen when I moved away from my parent's home to a live in job at a Christian conference centre

I was very nervous but made it through the first day, in the evening we went to a Christian concert with Adrian Snell and one of the songs touched me deeply and that evening I went home and listened to it in my room and I felt peace, then I got two sentences in my mind and they kept rolling around in my brain and would not go away so I decide to write them down and that is when the rest of it came and my new poem was born and so was a gift that is precious to me and stayed with me for over 30 years

I won't say it has been an easy ride but I have always known the Love of Jesus in my life even when I walked away for a year he never left my side.

So here am I, and I would like to share, with you the poems that the Lord has blessed me with, I pray that they will touch your hearts, and encourage you and maybe even challenge you, but my biggest prayer, and hope is that the Glory, Honor and Praise goes to my everlasting Savior Lord and King

This book is based on a theme and that is my journey from not believing in God, and how through my experiences they have led me to a point trust. It is in sections according to the state I was in at the time. It can be read as a journey or you can just dip in where ever you want

OTHER BOOKS BY JULIE CLARK

Journey into hope

Coming series of books

I am your joy

I am your hope

I am your love

I am your strength

And also

The I am statements of Jesus

If you enjoyed this book or found it useful I'd be very grateful if you'd post a short review on Amazon. Your support really does make a difference and I read all the reviews personally so I can get your feedback and make this book even better.

If you'd like to leave a review then all you need to do is click the review link on this book's page on Amazon here: Thanks again for your support!

Printed in Great Britain
by Amazon.co.uk, Ltd.,
Marston Gate.